Boats

Teaching Tips

Blue Level 4

This book focuses on the phonemes **/or/ /ur/**.

Before Reading

- Discuss the title. Ask readers what they think the book will be about. Have them briefly explain why.
- Ask readers to sort the words on page 3. Read the sounds and words together.

Read the Book

- Encourage readers to break down unfamiliar words into units of sound. Then, ask them to string the sounds together to create the words.
- Urge readers to point out when the focused phonics phonemes appear in the text.

After Reading

- Encourage children to reread the book independently or with a friend.
- Ask readers to name other words with /or/ or /ur/ phonemes. On a separate sheet of paper, have them write the words.

© 2024 Booklife Publishing
This edition is published by arrangement with Booklife Publishing.

North American adaptations © 2024 Jump!
5357 Penn Avenue South
Minneapolis, MN 55419
www.jumplibrary.com

Decodables by Jump! are published by Jump! Library.
All rights reserved. No part of this book may be reproduced in any form without written permission from the publisher.

Library of Congress Cataloging-in-Publication Data is available at www.loc.gov or upon request from the publisher.

ISBN: 979-8-88524-736-8 (hardcover)
ISBN: 979-8-88524-737-5 (paperback)
ISBN: 979-8-88524-738-2 (ebook)

Photo Credits

Images are courtesy of Shutterstock.com. With thanks to Getty Images, Thinkstock Photo and iStockphoto. Cover - 4&5 - Olga Donchuk, Melanie Lonbeck. 6&7 – 365 Focus Photography, Olga Lyubkin. 8&9 – tridland, lunamarina, 10&11 – South Bay Lee, Triff, 12&13 – Galina Barskaya, 14&15 – atk work, Valeriy Lebedev. 16 – Shutterstock.

Can you sort the words on this page into two groups?

Port

Turn

Sort

For

Surf

Horn

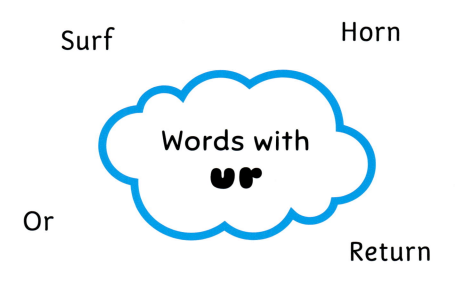

Or

Return

All sorts of boats are at this port. Can you see them all?

This boat is at the port. It has lots of horns for the dark and the fog.

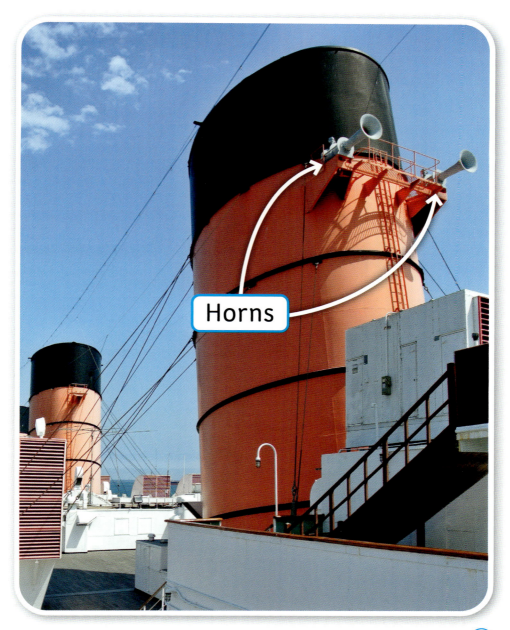

Horns

Boats can be big. This boat is big and long.

This boat is not big. It can fit a kid in it.

Boats can be for a lot of things.
They can be for fun or for jobs.

This sailboat is for fun. It has big sails.

This is a tugboat. It is not big.

Tugboat

It can tug things. It can tug a big boat and get it to turn.

Get the rope! This boat can tug a man. He can surf.

This kid can surf too. Look at her go!

Get the anchor! It is your turn to toss it.

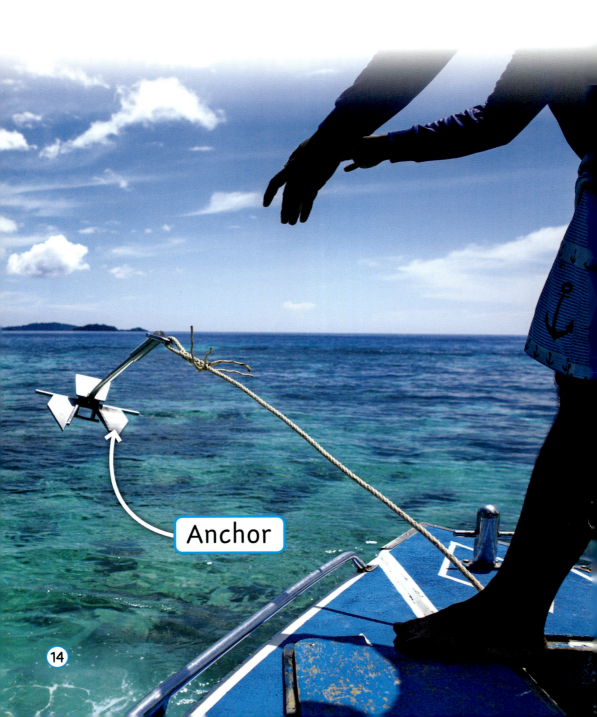

Anchor

It is dark and hard to see. The lights are for us to see.

Sound out each word. Does it have an /or/ or /ur/ sound?

corn

turtle

fur

fork